L Is for LION

And Other Playful Alphabet Fun

Between the Lions Staff

Bulk purchase

Gryphon House books are available for special premiums and sales promotions as well as for fund-raising use. Special editions or book excerpts also can be created to specification. For details, contact the Director of Marketing at Gryphon House.

Disclaimer

And Other
Playful
Alphabet
Fun

L Is for LION

by the *Between the Lions*® Staff

Based on the Award-Winning PBS KIDS® Literacy Series

BETWEEN THE LIONS is funded in part by The Corporation for Public Broadcasting, a cooperative agreement from the U.S. Department of Education's Ready To Learn grant, and by the Barksdale Reading Institute.

Corporation
for Public
Broadcasting
A private corporation funded by
the American people

BARKSDALE READING INSTITUTE

BETWEEN THE LIONS is produced by WGBH Boston, Sirius Thinking, Ltd., and Mississippi Public Broadcasting.

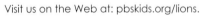

Mississippi
Public
Broadcasting

Visit us on the Web at: pbskids.org/lions.

Printed in China.

Published by Gryphon House, Inc.
10770 Columbia Pike, Suite 201, Silver Spring, MD 20901
301.595.9500; 301.595.0051 (fax); 800.638.0928 (toll-free)
Visit us on the web at www.gryphonhouse.com.

Library of Congress Cataloging-in-Publication Information
L is for lion: and other playful alphabet fun.
    p. cm.
ISBN 978-0-87659-354-7

Table of Contents

L Is for LION

Introduction

Learning the names, shapes, and sounds of letters has never been so much fun!

The activities, games, information, and ideas in this book were developed by the staff of *Between the Lions*, the award-winning PBS KIDS television series, which is produced by WGBH Boston, Sirius Thinking, Ltd., and Mississippi Public Broadcasting. The television series features a lion family—parents Theo and Cleo and their cubs, Lionel and Leona—who live in a public library. This book uses the same playful approach as the *Between the Lions* program, in which the doors "between the lions" swing open to reveal a place in which characters pop off the pages of books, letters sing, and words come alive.

Between the Lions has been the subject of numerous independent, scientifically-based reading research studies that have all shown that the program has a significant impact on increasing children's literacy. For more information about the *Between the Lions* program and for more literacy games and activities, go to pbskids.org/lions.

Open the pages of this book and find lively, fun-to-do ideas that will help your child begin to learn the alphabet by searching for letters in a newspaper, singing a song, marching along the shape of a letter, and lots more. Let the fun (and learning) begin!

Letters and the Sounds They Make

Try the following fun and easy ideas to help your child learn to recognize the letters of the alphabet and the sound each letter makes.

- Say the name of your child's favorite toy or food. What is the first letter of that word? Ask your child to point to it on an alphabet chart, in a book, on a food package, or on a sign. What sound does the letter make?
- Talk about the shapes of certain letters. Say, *I think the letter S looks like a snake. M looks like two mountains. T looks like a telephone pole.*
- Use your fingers, arms, or whole body to make letter shapes. Ask your child to make the letters T, L, and O. Together, can you make the letters H and A?

In *L Is for Lion*, when we talk about the sound that a letter makes, it appears between two slashes. For example, the letter S makes the /s/ sound.

Introduction

- How did you learn the alphabet? Probably by singing "The Alphabet Song"! Sing the song with your child. Sing it slowly and sing it quickly. Whisper it or shout it out loud! Sing it forward and then sing it backward!

The Alphabet Song
A – B – C – D – E – F – G,
H – I – J – K – L – M – N – O – P,
Q – R – S,
T – U – V,
W – X,
Y and Z,
Now I know my ABCs.
Next time sing them backward with me.

The Alphabet Song Backward
Z – Y – X – W – V – U – T,
S – R – Q – P – O – N – M – L – K,
J – I – H,
G – F – E,
D – C,
B and A,
Now I've said my ZYX's.
Bet that's not what you expected!

- If you have alphabet magnets on your refrigerator, your child may enjoy matching the magnetic letters to the letters on the pages of this book.
  Note: If you are unfamiliar with this song or any other song in this book, use a search engine to find places on the web where you can hear it.

Your Child's Name

Your child's first name is a very important word. In fact, it's the perfect word to help your child learn about letters and the sounds they make.

- Write your child's name on lunch bags, in a sandbox, on foggy windows, and on mirrors. Say the letters aloud as you write. Invite your child to write too!
- Together, make the letters of your child's name from objects such as twigs and pipe cleaners or from clay or cookie dough.
- Search for things that begin with the same sound as your child's name. Make up a song together with lots of verses.
  What begins with T? What begins with T?
  Tanya and table both begin with T.
- Look for the first letter of your child's name on signs, food packages, and magazine covers. Look for other favorite letters. Point to and say the first letter of your name, too. What other letters can your child name?
- Read alphabet books together (a few suggestions follow), and then make an alphabet book! For each letter, think of a family name or something that your child likes. Together with your child, draw a picture on a piece of paper (or attach a photo). Write a word or sentence on the paper about the picture. Soon you will have your own alphabet book.

Books About the Alphabet

The ABCs of Fruits and Vegetables and Beyond by Steve Charney

This alphabet book includes jokes, tongue twisters, unusual facts, poems, kid-friendly recipes, shopping tips, and more to interest kids in nutritious foods.

The Alphabet Tree by Leo Lionni

Wordbug, the main character in *The Alphabet Tree,* teaches the alphabet letters how to become stronger by banding together to form words.

Alphabet Under Construction by Denise Fleming

In *Alphabet Under Construction,* a playful mouse builds all the letters of the alphabet, letter by letter, using different tools and materials.

Chicka Chicka Boom Boom by Bill Martin Jr. and John Archambault

In this alphabet book, letters race up a coconut tree. This book is fun to read because it has lots of rhyming words.

From Anne to Zach by Mary Jane Martin

Identify the letters of the alphabet as you learn 26 names from Anne to Olaf to Quent to Uri.

K Is for Kissing a Cool Kangaroo by Giles Andreae

This alphabet book features an amusing combination of objects and animals on each letter page, with delightful rhyming text.

The Letters Are Lost! by Lisa Campbell Ernst

This book is about a set of alphabet blocks that are all together one day—all neat and put away in the right place. Then, one by one, the blocks disappear. Soon, all the alphabet blocks have disappeared. The alphabet block box is empty. There's nothing in it. The letters are lost!

Mrs. McTats and Her House Full of Cats by Alyssa Satin Capucilli

Mrs. McTats starts off with a cat named Abner, but ends up with 24 more and a puppy named Zoom.

The Vegetable Alphabet Book by Jerry Pallotta and Bob Thomson

Graze through the alphabet in this fun, fact-filled book that begins with asparagus and ends with zucchetta.

What Pete Ate from A to Z by Maira Kalman

Pete the dog eats an accordion and then a variety of outrageous items in alphabetical order.

Word Play

As children begin to recognize letters and their sounds (part of learning to read), they need to "sound out" words. Playing with rhymes (words that end with the same sound) and poems helps children understand how words are made up of sounds and how changing the first sound can make a new word: book, look, cook.

Don't be afraid to get silly and use nonsense words! As children play with words, they become more aware of the sounds of language and the way those sounds can be put together.

- Make up rhymes using your child's name: Jenna, Benna, Fenna.
- Teach your child fingerplays and hand-clapping rhymes, such as "Patty Cake."
- Sing songs together. Sing in the car or while waiting in line.
- Read a rhyming book. Try one of the following:
  Green Eggs and Ham by Dr. Seuss
  Kevin and His Dad by Irene Smalls
  One Duck Stuck by Phyllis Root

Look for Click the Mouse!

Click the Mouse is a character on the award-winning show *Between the Lions*. When she appears on the show, something remarkable happens! Click the Mouse and the website address of **pbskids.org/lions/gryphonhouse** appear on some of the alphabet pages of *L Is for Lion*, followed by listings of stories, poems, songs, video clips, and/or games related to that letter.

Sequence of Learning About Letters and Their Sounds

In general, children learn about the names, shapes, and sounds of the letters of the alphabet in the following sequence. Your child will:

- Begin to recognize letters
- Recognize his or her first name in print
- Understand that the alphabet is made up of letters and that each has a different name
- Distinguish letter shapes (straight line, curvy line, slanted line, and so on)
- Associate names of letters with their shapes
- Notice the beginning letters in familiar words
- Identify the first letter in a word
- Associate the names of letters with their sounds

Aa

Eat an A

Enjoy the taste of apricots, apples, avocados, applesauce, or any other food beginning with the letter A. Say the name of each food, emphasizing the short /a/ sound.

Move Like an Alligator

Move on your belly like an alligator. Mention that the word *alligator* begins with the letter A, which makes the short /a/ sound.

Walk an A

Draw the outline of the letter A on the floor with tape or chalk. Show your child how to walk along the lines of the letter A. As she walks, teach your child words that begin with the letter A. Encourage her to repeat the words after you say them.

Write an A

To help your child learn how to write the uppercase letter A, draw the letter in the air. As you draw the lines in the air (first the slanted line on the left, next the slanted line on the right, and last the horizontal line connecting the two slanted lines), ask your child to do the same motions. Practice writing the letter A in the air, and then show your child how to write the letter A on paper.

Read *The Letters Are Lost!* by Lisa Campbell Ernst before or after searching for letters, or read *Abiyoyo* by Pete Seeger, emphasizing all the short /a/ sounds in the book.

Introducing Vowels

As a song featured on *Between the Lions* points out, you "Can't Make a Word without a Vowel"—the letters a-e-i-o-u and sometimes y. And unlike most consonants, vowels have multiple sounds. All vowels have a "short" vowel sound, like the /a/ in *cap*, and a "long" sound like /ay/ in *cape* or *train*. They can make a different sound next to an *r* as in *barn* or no sound at all, like the *a* in *team*. The sounds of vowels are often harder to learn than the sounds of consonants. This is a skill you can focus on after your child knows the consonant sounds.

Letter Hunt

What You Will Need

plastic letters or wooden alphabet blocks

What to Do

- Set up a letter hunt and then challenge your child to find the As that are "lost."
- Hide letter A alphabet blocks or plastic letters around the room. (You may want to place letters on or near an object that begins with the letter A. For instance, place one of the alphabet blocks or plastic letters near an apple, an arrow, or a toy alligator.)
- Explain that a strange thing has happened. The first letter of the alphabet, the letter A, has disappeared!
- Help your child go on a hunt to find all the lost letters.

More Ideas

Three Words for You

Challenge your child to hear the /a/ sound in words such as *apple, arrow,* and *alphabet.* Say three words, two that begin with the letter A and one that begins with a different letter. For example, say, *apple, arrow, bubble.* Ask your child to clap when she hears a word that begins with the sound of the letter A. Repeat with three new words. Once she understands how to play, ask her to say three words for you.

> **Note:** Focus on the short /a/ sound first. Introduce the long /a/ sound (in words such as *acorn* and *ape*) once your child can recognize the short /a/ sound.

Find an A

Give your child a page from a newspaper, a magazine, or a catalog that has large type. Suggest that she use a marker to circle all the As on the page.

Aa

Letter A Vocabulary

acorn
alligator
alphabet
ape
apple
arrow
ask
asleep
at
awake
away

Click the Mouse!

For more fun with the letter A, check out pbskids.org/lions/gryphonhouse.

Songs:	**Can't Make a Word without a Vowel**
	Get Your Mouth Moving (a)
	If You Can Read: at
Video Clips:	**Opposite Bunny: asleep/awake**
	Vowel Boot Camp (man/main)
Games:	**ABCD Watermelon**
	Dub Cubs

Bb

Bees and Butterflies
Flutter your arms and buzz around like a bee, or listen to soft music and move like a butterfly to the music.

Yummy Bs
Enjoy the taste of burritos, bananas, beans, beets, and berries. Name each food, emphasizing the /b/ sound.

Wrap Your Tongue Around the Letter B
Say the following tongue twister, emphasizing the /b/ sounds:

*Betty bought a bit of butter
But said she, "This butter's bitter.
If I put it in my batter,
It will make my batter bitter."
So Betty bought a bit of better butter
And put it in her batter,
And it made her batter better.*

Read Bee-bim Bop! by Linda Sue Park, Beetle Bop by Denise Fleming, or What's in the Box? by Bill Gillham, emphasizing all the /b/ sounds as you read.

Buzzing Around
Practice making the /b/ sound. It's fun to say, *Bees and butterflies like to buzz around*, because the sentence has lots of /b/ sounds. Say the words again slowly, emphasizing the /b/ sound. Ask, *Can you hear the /b/ sound?* Say the word *bee* again, emphasizing the initial /b/ sound: *bbbbee!*

Button Sort

What You Will Need

buttons in a variety of shapes, sizes, and colors
clean, empty egg carton

What to Do

- Display a variety of buttons. Explain that the word *button* begins with the letter B, which makes the sound /b/. Say *button*, emphasizing the /b/ sound, bbbbbutton.
- Hold up one of the buttons and help your child describe it. Ask, *How many holes does this button have? What color is this button? What shape is this button? What is this button made out of?*
- Talk about different ways to sort the buttons, and then model how to sort the buttons into the sections of an empty egg carton.
- Ask, *Can you think of another way to sort the buttons?* Let your child use his own categories for sorting the buttons.

More Ideas

Sounds Like B

Display a bag or bucket, along with small items that begin with the /b/ sound, such as a ball, button, block, and book, and a few items that do not begin with the /b/ sound (crayon, fork, toy car). Name each item. Explain that only things that begin with the /b/ sound belong in the bucket. Hold up the ball and ask, *Does the word* ball *begin with the /b/ sound? Yes, it begins with the /b/ sound. Let's put the ball into the bucket.* Pick up another object, name it, and then ask your child if it belongs in the bucket. Continue until all the items have been sorted.

Eat the Bears!

Roll out refrigerated sugar cookie dough, or make your own cookie dough. Have your child help you roll out the dough. Use a bear-shaped cookie cutter to cut out cookies or use a knife to cut out a bear face—a large round face with two small round ears. Bake and enjoy the bears! **Note:** Wash hands before making the cookies.

Bb

Click the Mouse!
For more fun with the letter B, check out pbskids.org/lions/gryphonhouse.

Stories: Bee-bim Bop!
Beetle Bop
Video Clips: If You Were: beetle
Play with Words: butterfly
un People: buttoned/unbuttoned

Letter B
Vocabulary
baby
bag
ball
banana
barn
bat
beans
bear
bed
bee
bell
berries
bird
block
boat
book
box
boy
bucket
butter
butterfly
bug
button

····· Letter Bb ·····

Cc

Eat a C

Enjoy the taste of carrots, corn, cantaloupe, cucumbers, cake, cocoa, or any other food beginning with the letter C. Say the name of each food, emphasizing the /k/ sound.

C Patterns

Arrange slices of carrots and cucumbers into a pattern, such as carrot, carrot, cucumber, carrot, carrot, cucumber. Ask your child to continue the pattern or create her own pattern. Create a new pattern by eating slices of cucumbers or carrots. (Eat a carrot slice to change the pattern of carrot, carrot, cucumber to carrot, cucumber.)

Move Like a Cat or a Caterpillar

Slink like a cat, with your back curled up and your hands and knees on the floor, or crawl on your belly like a caterpillar.

Caterpillar Crackers

Place a piece of lettuce on a plate. Spread peanut butter or cream cheese onto three or more crackers. Create a caterpillar body by overlapping three or more crackers on top of the lettuce. Count the crackers. Add raisins for eyes and thin pretzel sticks for feelers. Eat and enjoy your caterpillar cracker!

Read *The Carrot Seed* by Crocket Johnson or *Click, Clack, Moo: Cows That Type* by Doreen Cronin, emphasizing the /k/ sound as you read.

Click the Mouse!
For more fun with the letter C, check out pbskids.org/lions/gryphonhouse.

Stories:	A Birthday for Cow!
	City Mouse and Country Mouse
Songs:	City Country Rap
	The Two Sounds Made by c
Poem:	Caterpillar
Video Clip:	If You Were: cat

Guess the Animal

What You Will Need

pictures of a cow, cat, and caterpillar

> **Note:** Magazines and catalogs are good places to find pictures. If you have access to a computer, search for the pictures you need and print them out.

What to Do

- Tell your child that you are thinking of a certain animal.
- Say that you are going to give her hints about the animal, and she should guess what the animal is.

  > **Note:** To confirm your child's guess, show her a picture of the animal.

- Say, *I'm thinking of an animal that begins with the /k/ sound. This animal gives us milk and says "Moo." Can you guess what it is?* (cow)
- Say, *I'm thinking of another animal that begins with the /k/ sound. This animal has soft fur and says "Meow." Can you guess what it is?* (cat)
- Say, *I'm thinking of another animal that begins with the /k/ sound. This animal wiggles on the ground. It turns into a butterfly. Can you guess what it is?* (caterpillar)

More Ideas

What Is the Sound?

Select objects or pictures of objects and animals that begin with the /k/ sound (for example, candy, car, cat, cookie, corn, cow). Name the objects or pictures, emphasizing the sound /k/ of the letter C, and then say, *Cat, cow, car, candy—can you hear the /k/ sound at the beginning of these words? The letter C makes the /k/ sound.*

> **Note:** Once your child is familiar with the /k/ sound, explain that the letter C actually makes two sounds—a hard C, which sounds like /k/, and soft C, which sounds like /s/. Then play this game with words that begin with the soft C (/s/ sound), like *celery, cereal, circus, circle,* and *city*.

Color Collage

Explain and model the process of making a green collage. Say, *The word* collage *begins with the letter C and the /k/ sound.* Explain that a collage is a piece of art made by gluing different objects and shapes onto a piece of paper. Think aloud as you select green objects and shapes to arrange on a piece of construction paper. Say, *I think this green button would look nice here. I think I'll put this green square here.* Once you have arranged your items on the paper, show your child how to glue them into place. Show your child how to add more green with green crayons, markers, or paint. On another day, create a color collage using another color, or create a rainbow collage.

Cc

Dd

D Is for Dance

Draw the outline of the uppercase letter D on the floor with tape or chalk. Play quiet music and have your child dance on tiptoes along the lines of the letter. Then, play music with a strong beat and suggest that your child dance to the beat of the music along the lines of the letter.

I'm Thinking of a Word

Play a guessing game with your child to help him hear and identify the /d/ sound in the beginning of familiar words. Say, *I am thinking of a word that begins with the /d/ sound, like the word dog. It is something that you open and shut when you walk into a house or a room.* Wait for your child to suggest an answer. Respond, *Yes! door.*

Roll the Dice

Play with a set of dice or one die. Take turns guessing which number you will roll.

Read *Not Afraid of Dogs* by Susanna Pitzer, "The Camel Dances" from *Fables* by Arnold Lobel, *How to Be a Good Dog* by Gail Page, or *One Duck Stuck* by Phyllis Root, emphasizing the /d/ sound as you read.

Rhymes
Featuring the Letter D

Recite, chant, or sing the following nonsense nursery rhymes that feature the letter D. Emphasize the /d/ sound each time the letter D appears in a word.

Hey, Diddle, Diddle

*Hey, diddle, diddle,
The cat and the fiddle,
The cow jumped over the moon.
The little dog laughed to see such a sight,
And the dish ran away with the spoon.*

Dickery, Dickery, Dare

*Dickery, dickery, dare,
The pig flew up in the air.
The man in brown
Soon brought him down!
Dickery, dickery, dare.*

D Dot

What You Will Need

circle stickers and/or ink pads with washable ink
dots from a hole punch or circles of confetti
poster board
scissors
tape

What to Do

- Cut out a large uppercase D from poster board.
- Lightly tape the letter cutout onto a table.
- Have your child decorate the letter with dots. Your child can glue a line of confetti or hole-punch dots on the cutout or make dots using circle stickers or fingerprints (pressing one finger on an ink pad).
- Chant *dot, dot, dot* as your child makes the dots, emphasizing the initial /d/ sound of the word dot. Encourage your child to say it with you. If your child is using stickers or ink pads that come in two colors, he can make and chant a color pattern, red dot, blue dot; red dot, blue dot.

More Ideas

Labels, Labels, Everywhere

Tape the word door onto a door at your child's eye level. As you attach the word, ask your child to repeat the word with you. Point out the letter d at the beginning of the word. Repeat with *desk, doorknob, doll, toy dog (or dinosaur),* and *drum*.

What Is Your Dream Cake?

Ask your child to imagine what his dream cake would look like. What shape would it be? What kind of icing would it have? What kind of decorations? Would there be any writing on it? What would the writing say? Have your child use a round or square piece of paper and art materials to create his dream cake. Help write any letters or words your child would like to put on the cake.

Click the Mouse!
For more fun with the letter D, check out pbskids.org/lions/gryphonhouse.

Stories:	How to Be a Good Dog
	Not Afraid of Dogs
Song:	Delighted You're Mine
Video Clip:	Blending Bowl: dine

Dd

Letter D Vocabulary

dance
deer
dice
dine
dinosaur
dog
doll
donut
dragonfly
dream
drum
duck
dump truck

Ee

Put Your E in the Air

Tell your child that she should listen for the word elbow in your "Simon Says" directions. For example, when you say, Simon Says, *"Put your elbow in the air (or on your knee,)"* your child should follow that direction. However, your child should not move when you say, Simon Says, *"Put your arm in the air."* Let your child have a chance to give "Simon Says" directions.

Paint an E

Draw a large outline of the uppercase letter E on paper. Suggest that your child use paint to fill in the outline of the letter. Help your child notice that the letter E is written with four straight lines.

Eat an E

Shape bread dough into letter E shapes. Bake and eat. What a yummy E!

Move Like an Elephant

Show your child how to let one of her arms hang down from her mouth to make a "trunk." Walk around the room while chanting the following rhyme. Emphasize the short sound of the letter E in the word *elephant*.

Read *Eating the Alphabet* by Lois Ehlert, *An Egg Is Quiet* by Dianna Hutts Aston, or *Elephants Can Paint Too!* by Katya Arnold, emphasizing the /e/ sound as you read.

One Elephant
One elephant went out to play,
Out on a spider's web one day.
He had such enormous fun,
He called for another elephant to come.

Repeat for two elephants, three elephants, and so on.

Shape the Letter E

Note: You can make a letter card by writing the uppercase and lowercase letter on an index card.

What You Will Need

letter card that shows both the uppercase E and lowercase e
modeling clay, pipe cleaners, or another modeling material

What to Do

- Display a letter card with both the uppercase E and lowercase e on it.
- Trace both the uppercase E and lowercase e letters on the card and then draw the letters in the air.
- Point out that the uppercase and lowercase letters have different shapes.
  Note: You might want to show your child a letter, such as C, which has uppercase and lowercase letters that are the same shape.
- Ask your child to use clay, pipe cleaners, or another material to make the shapes of uppercase E and lowercase e.
- As you look at the shape of each letter and as your child shapes the letters, use words like *straight* and *curved* to describe the letters.

Another Idea

Apples, Bananas, and Vowels

The following chant is a fun way to learn the long sounds of vowels. Chant it with your child. Emphasize the third verse.

Apples and Bananas

I like to eat, eat, eat apples and bananas.
I like to eat, eat, eat apples and bananas.

I like to ate, ate, ate ay-ples and bay-nay-nays.
I like to ate, ate, ate ay-ples and bay-nay-nays.

I like to eat, eat, eat ee-ples and bee-nee-nees.
I like to eat, eat, eat ee-ples and bee-nee-nees.

I like to ite, ite, ite i-ples and by-ny-nys.
I like to ite, ite, ite i-ples and by-ny-nys.

I like to ote, ote, ote oh-ples and bo-no-nos.
I like to ote, ote, ote oh-ples and bo-no-nos.

I like to ute, ute, ute up-ples and bu-nu-nus.
I like to ute, ute, ute up-ples and bu-nu-nus.

Ee

Letter E Vocabulary

eagle
ear
egg
eggplant
elbow
elephant
elevator
elk
enchilada

Click the Mouse!
For more fun with the letter E, check out pbskids.org/lions/gryphonhouse.

Stories:	An Egg Is Quiet	Elephants Can Paint Too!
Songs:	Double e, ee	If You Can read: en
	Sven Said	
Video Clips:	Fred Says: elephant	If You Were: eagle
Game:	Dub Cubs	

Ff

Eat an F Every Day!

Try a new food beginning with the letter F, such as figs, fudge, or fettuccine.

Put an F in the Air!

Use your hand to write an uppercase F and a lowercase f in the air. This will help your child recognize and begin to "write" the letter F. When tracing the lowercase letter f, tell your child to start by making a walking cane or a candy cane.

F Moves Like This

Slink like a fox or swim like a fish. Mention that both animals begin with the letter F, which makes the /f/ sound.

F, F, F, Feelings

Say the following poem, emphasizing the /f/ sound that the letter F makes each time you say the words *feelings* and *fast*.

Feelings

Feelings come and feelings go,
Sometimes fast and sometimes slow.
Sometimes happy, sometimes sad,
Sometimes silly, sometimes mad.
Feelings come and feelings go,
Like an afternoon rainbow.

Read *When I Was Five* by Arthur Howard or *Chicks and Salsa* by Aaron Reynolds, emphasizing the /f/ sound as you read.

Foot to Foot

What You Will Need

no materials needed

What to Do

- Ask, *Can you name a part of your body that begins with the letter F?* (foot, finger)
- Point to your foot or your finger.
- Tell your child to touch that part of his body to the same part of your body. For example, little finger to little finger or foot to foot.
- There are many ways to follow these directions. For example, they can be done sitting or standing, with arms up or arms down, or any other way that is fun to do.

More Ideas

Finger Family

Do the following fingerplay, emphasizing the /f/ sound in each word.

Finger Family

Finger family up, (Hold out your hands in fists; stretch fingers up.)
And finger family down. (Hold out hands in fists; stretch fingers down.)
Finger family dancing,
All around the town. (Wiggle and dance fingers in a circle.)
Dance them on your shoulders, (Dance fingers on shoulders.)
Dance them on your head. (Dance fingers on head.)
Dance them on your knees, (Dance fingers on knees.)
And tuck them into bed. (Tuck hands into your armpits.)

Feelings Collage

Help your child find pictures of faces that show different feelings and then use the pictures to create a collage. The pictures in the collage can show one feeling, such as a "Happy Collage," or a variety of feelings. **Note:** Magazines and catalogs are good places to find pictures. If you have access to a computer, search for the pictures you need and print them out.

Click the Mouse!
For more fun with the letter F, check out pbskids.org/lions/gryphonhouse.

Stories:	Hide-and-Seek
	Sea Horse
Song:	Fabulous
Video Clip:	Fred Says: fish

Ff

Letter F
Vocabulary
fabulous
face
fairy
fan
farm
fast
feather
feelings
fettuccine
fig
firefly
fish
foot
football
fork
fox
fudge
fun
fur
fuzzy

Gg

G Is for Goose

Use tape or chalk to write an uppercase G and a lowercase g on the floor or on a sidewalk. Suggest that your child honk like a goose (a word that begins with the letter G, which has the /g/ sound) as she walks along the lines of the letters. Ask your child what she notices about the uppercase and lowercase letters. Do they have the same shape or a different shape?

How Does Your Garden Grow?

Chant the following nursery rhyme, emphasizing the /g/ sound in the word garden.

Mary, Mary

Mary, Mary, quite contrary,
How does your garden grow?
With silver bells and cockle shells,
And pretty maids all in a row.

Two Sounds for the Letter G

Explain to your child that the letter G makes the hard /g/ sound. Repeat the word *garden* with your child, emphasizing the initial hard /g/ sound (gggarden). Tell your child that the letter G is a special letter. Sometimes it sounds like a hard /g/, as in the words *garden* and *girl*. But sometimes it sounds soft like a /j/, as in the words *gym*, *giraffe*, and *gingerbread*.

Read *Good Night, Gorilla* by Peggy Rathmann, emphasizing the /g/ sound as you read, or *Giraffes Can't Dance* by Giles Andreae, emphasizing the /j/ sound as you read.

Click the Mouse!
For more fun with the letter G, check out pbskids.org/lions/gryphonhouse.
Story: Chicks and Salsa
Song: The Two Sounds Made by g
Poem: You Never Hear the Garden Grow

Gingerbread Man Shapes

What You Will Need

bread
cream cheese or frosting
dried fruit, sunflower seeds, and/or candy
gingerbread man (or woman) cookie cutter

What to Do

- Use the cookie cutter to cut gingerbread man shapes out of slices of bread.
- Spread cream cheese onto the shapes and use dried fruit, sunflower seeds, or candies to decorate each gingerbread man.
- Enjoy the yummy gingerbread man shapes.
- As you eat the gingerbread man shapes, ask, *What part of your gingerbread man do you eat first—the head, arm, or leg?*
  Note: Remember to wash your hands before beginning this project.

More Ideas

Gingerbread Cookies

Mix your favorite recipe to make gingerbread boy (or girl) cookies or buy gingerbread boy (or girl) cookies. Have your child decorate them using cream cheese or frosting, dried fruit, sunflower seeds, and/or candies.

Gingerbread Children

Ask your child to tell you a story about one of her gingerbread cookies. Ask, *What is your cookie's name? What does your cookie like to do? How is your cookie feeling?*

Match Gingerbread Children

Use a gingerbread boy (or girl) cookie cutter to cut out 12 identical brown paper gingerbread people. Add simple decorations to make six matching pairs. Use buttons, happy or sad faces, and decorations at the wrists and ankles (zigzag lines, straight lines, or no lines) to make distinct pairs. Model how to find a matching pair and place them together. Then let your child find the matching pairs.

Gg

Letter G Vocabulary

garden
gift
gingerbread
giraffe
girl
goat
gopher
goose
gorilla
gum
gym

Hh

Tasty Hs

Explore the taste of food that begins with the letter H, such as hot chocolate, honeydew, hot dogs, or hamburgers.

Use Your Hand

Place your hand near your mouth. Say words that begin with the letter H, emphasizing the first sound, such as *hhhhot* or *hhhhat*. Ask your child how the sound of the letter H feels on his hand, another word that begins with the letter H, which makes the /h/ sound.

Walk Like an H

Use tape or chalk to write an uppercase H and a lowercase h on the floor or on a sidewalk. Encourage your child to learn about the shape of the letter by walking along the lines.

Read *Hippopotamus* by Patricia Whitehouse; *A House Is a House for Me* by Mary Ann Hoberman; *Houses and Homes* by Ann Morris; *Hats, Hats, Hats* by Ann Morris; or *The Little Red Hen* by various authors, including Byron Barton, Jerry Pinkney, and Paul Galdone. Emphasize the /h/ sound in each story.

Sounds Like H to Me!

Chant the following nursery rhymes that feature the /h/ sound of the letter H.

Hickory, Dickory, Dock!

Hickory, dickory, dock!
The mouse ran up the clock;
The clock struck one,
The mouse ran down,
Hickory, dickory, dock!

Humpty Dumpty

Humpty Dumpty sat on
*   the wall,*
Humpty Dumpty had a
*   great fall.*
All the king's horses
And all the king's men
Couldn't put Humpty
*   Dumpty*
Together again.

Simon Says /h/

What You Will Need
no materials needed

What to Do
- Tell your child, or a group of children, that in this game of Simon Says, they are to do what you say only if they hear the /h/ sound.
- If they don't hear the /h/ sound, they should stand still with their hands at their sides. Have the children repeat the following /h/ words with you: *hair, head, hips, hop, hug, hum.*
- Say, *Simon Says touch your head.* Emphasize the /h/ sound in the word *head.* Ask, *Did you hear the /h/ sound? Yes! Touch your head.*
- Repeat with the words *hair, nose, hips,* and *ears.*
- Say, *Simon says hop. Did you hear the /h/ sound? Hop!*
- Repeat with the words *hug, sing,* and *hum.*

More Ideas
Feel the Letters
Write an uppercase H and lowercase h on separate index cards. Suggest that your child squeeze glue along the outlines of the letters and then sprinkle sand or glitter on the lines of glue. When the glue dries, encourage your child to trace the outline of the letters with his finger to learn the shapes of uppercase H and lowercase h.

Helping Hands
Help your child trace the outline of his hand onto a piece of construction paper. Cut along the outline and ask your child to dictate a sentence about one way he can use his hand to help you (or anyone else). Point to each word as you read the dictation aloud. Help your child write his name on his handprint. Make another handprint and write on it another way your child uses his hand to help. Use glue or tape to make a collage of all his helping hands.

Click the Mouse!
For more fun with the letter H, check out pbskids.org/lions/gryphonhouse.
Story:	The Happy Hocky Family Moves to the Country!
Songs:	Humongous
	Hung Up on h
	My House
Video Clips:	Fred says: hot
	If You Were: hippopotamus

Hh

Letter H Vocabulary
hair
hamburger
hand
happy
hat
head
heart
helicopter
hen
hippopotamus
hips
honey
honeydew
hop
horn
horse
hot
hot chocolate
hot dog
house
hum
humongous

Ii

One Inch, Two Inches

Show your child how a ruler is marked in inches, a word that begins with the letter I, which makes the /i/ sound. Use the ruler to measure a few common objects, such as a block, a book, and a spoon. Once your child understands the concept of measuring objects, ask her to guess the length, in inches, of different objects, such as a knife, a doll, or a magazine.

The Same as Ice Cream

Show your child pictures of things that begin with the short and long vowel sounds of the letter I. For example, show her pictures of an igloo and ice cream. Name the things in the pictures and explain that they both begin with the letter I, which makes these two different beginning sounds. Now show her pictures of more things that begin with the /i/ sound of I (such as inchworm) and things that begin with long I (ice). Ask her, *Which pictures begin with the same short /i/ sound as igloo? Which begin with the same long /i/ sound as ice cream?*

Move Like Insects!

Talk with your child about insects, such as ants, bees, and grasshoppers. Ask your child to select an insect and then move how that insect moves. Point out that the word *insect* begins with the /i/ sound of the letter I.

Sing About I

Enjoy the following song that features the /i/ sound of the letter I in the words *itsy* and *bitsy,* and the long sound of I in the words *spider, climbed,* and *dried.*

Itsy Bitsy Spider

The itsy bitsy spider
Climbed up the waterspout
Down came the rain
And washed the spider out
Out came the sun
And dried up all the rain
Now the itsy bitsy spider
Climbed up the spout again.

Note: If you are unfamiliar with this song or any other song in this book, use a search engine to find places on the web where you can hear it.

Ice Castles

What You Will Need

half-gallon juice containers with their
   tops cut off
ice cube trays
plastic containers of assorted sizes

sand
sand box or dishpan
water

What to Do

- Fill ice cube trays and plastic containers with water and freeze them.
  Note: It is easier to remove ice from containers that have straight edges than from containers with curved edges.
- Place the ice forms into a sand box or large dishpan filled with sand. (Sand will coat the ice, and the ice blocks will stick together.)
- Build with the ice blocks.
- Ask, *How does the ice feel? What do you think will happen to the ice if we don't put it back into the freezer? Why?*

More Ideas

Ice Cream for One

Place ½ cup milk, 1 tablespoon sugar, and ¼ teaspoon vanilla in a small resealable bag and seal the bag. Place the small bag, about 3 tablespoons rock salt, and ice cubes in a large bag. Seal and shake. In a few minutes you will have ice cream for one!

The Little Word That Could

Write *it* on an index card. Point to the word and say, *It is an itsy-bitsy word. It only has two letters, i and t, but it is a very busy word. We use it all the time!* Say the following chant: *It can, it can. Oh, yes, it can!*

Read How Much Is That Doggie in the Window? by Iza Trapani and Bob Merrill, It's Mine! by Leo Lionni, I Love Animals by Flora McDonnell, or Today Is Monday by Eric Carle, emphasizing the sounds made by the letter I as you read.

Click the Mouse!
For more fun with the letter I, check out pbskids.org/lions/gryphonhouse.
Stories: Oh, Yes, It Can!
         What Instrument Does Alvin Play?
Song: Can't Make a Word without a Vowel

Ii

Letter I
Vocabulary
ice
ice cream
icicle
icing
iguana
in
inch
inchworm
insect
instrument
invitation
it

Jj

Move Like a J

Jump like a jackrabbit or run like a jaguar.

Be Quick!

Enjoy the following rhyme that features the /j/ sound of the letter J.

Jack, be nimble. Jack, be quick!
Jack, jump over the candlestick.
Jack, be nimble. Jack, be quick!
Jack, jump over the candlestick!

Sing Loudly and Sing Softly

Practicing the /j/ sound of the letter J has never been so much fun! Sing this song four times. The first time, sing the verse loudly, the second time, sing it softly, the third time, whisper it, and the fourth time, sing it silently by mouthing the words. At the end of each verse, sing the chorus very loudly.

John Jacob Jingleheimer Schmidt
John Jacob Jingleheimer Schmidt,
His name is my name too.
Whenever we go out,
The people always shout,
"There goes John Jacob Jingleheimer Schmidt!"
Chorus: Da da da da da da da! (Sing loudly.)

Another J Song

Emphasize the /j/ sound as you sing this song.

Rig-a-Jig-Jig
As I was walking down the street,
Down the street, down the street,
A very good friend I chanced to meet. Hi-ho, hi-ho, hi-ho.
Rig-a-jig-jig and away we go,
Away we go, away we go!
Rig-a-jig-jig and away we go, Hi-ho, hi-ho, hi-ho.

Note: If you are unfamiliar with this song or any other song in this book, use a search engine to find places on the web where you can hear it.

Junk Sculpture

What You Will Need

assorted junk (recyclable odds and ends)

broken toy or game parts

paint and paintbrushes

flat pieces of cardboard

small cardboard boxes

small tray or container filled with watered-down glue

What to Do

- Place an assortment of "junk" (see What You Will Need) on a table.
- Tell your child that he is going to recycle the junk by making a sculpture, which is a piece of art!
- If necessary, demonstrate the process. Use a piece of flat cardboard as a base. Select the pieces you want to work with. As you dip the bottom of the pieces into the glue and hold them together, talk about what you are doing. *I think I'll start with this box. I'll put this piece on top of it because I think it will look like a robot.*
- Your child may want to paint his finished pieces.

More Ideas

Shape That Dough!

Suggest that your child roll out playdough or clay into "snakes" and then shape them into an uppercase J and a lowercase j. If your child needs a model to follow, print the letters on an index card.

Bag of J Sounds

Play a sound game to help your child listen for and recognize the /j/ sound at the beginning of familiar words. Display a jacket along with other small items that begin with the /j/ sound, such as jewelry, a jump rope, and a jar. Include a few items that do not begin with the /j/ sound, such as a button, a hat, and a sock. Tell your child that only things that begin with the /j/ sound belong in the bag. Continue until all the items have been sorted.

Jj

Letter J Vocabulary

jacket
jackrabbit
jaguar
jam
jar
jelly
jet
jewelry
job
jog
joke
jolly
juice
jump
jump rope
junk

Read Jonathan and His Mommy by Irene Smalls; Julius, the Baby of the World by Kevin Henkes; Dear Juno by Soyung Pak; or Joseph Had a Little Overcoat by Simms Taback, emphasizing the /j/ sound as you read.

Click the Mouse!
For more fun with the letter J, check out pbskids.org/lions/gryphonhouse.

Stories:	Joseph Had a Little Overcoat
	Just What Mama Needs
Song:	A Very Fun Job
Video Clip:	Monkey Cheer: jog

Kk

Hop Like a Kangaroo

Draw the outline of the letter K on the floor with tape or chalk and hop like a kangaroo on the lines of the letter.

Tongue Twister

Try to say the following tongue twister three times without laughing!

The king kisses kittens.

Help your child create her own tongue twisters.

Play a Kazoo

Grab a kazoo and play along to your favorite songs.

Fill the K

Draw the outline of an uppercase K on a sheet of paper. Suggest that your child use a crayon or marker to trace the outline of the letter and then use art materials to decorate the letter.

Read *King Midas: The Golden Touch* by Demi, *Mrs. Katz and Tush* by Patricia Polacco, *Cows in the Kitchen* by Jean Crebbin, *Kevin and His Dad* by Irene Smalls, or *K Is for Kissing a Cool Kangaroo* by Giles Andreae, emphasizing the /k/ sound as you read.

····· L Is for LION ·····

"I Spy" the Letter K

What You Will Need

objects, or pictures of objects, that begin with the letter K, such as a key, a kazoo, or a toy kangaroo (or a picture of a kangaroo) **Note:** Magazines and catalogs are good places to find pictures of objects. If you have access to a computer, search for objects that begin with the letter K and print them out.

What to Do

- Explain the sound that the letter K makes. Say, *The letter K makes the /k/ sound.*
- Choose an object, or the picture of an object, that begins with that sound and is visible. Describe it, emphasizing the /k/ sound. For example, say,
  - *I spy something that is metal, opens doors, and begins with the /k/ sound.* (key)
  - *I spy a picture of something that is an animal that hops around and begins with the /k/ sound.* (picture of a kangaroo)

More Ideas

Kaleidoscope Collage

Show your child how to use a kaleidoscope. Suggest that she create a collage of what she sees when she looks through the kaleidoscope. Help your child cut out geometric shapes from different colors of construction paper and then glue the pieces of construction paper onto a piece of drawing paper in a design that resembles what she sees in the kaleidoscope.

Like K, not Like K

Place magnetic letters or letter blocks in a bag. Take out one letter at a time. Help your child determine if the letter is like a K (written with straight lines only) or not like a K (written with straight and curved lines, such as D and Q, or written with curved lines only, such as O and C).

Kk

Letter K Vocabulary
kale
kaleidoscope
kangaroo
kazoo
key
kick
kidney beans
king
kiss
kite
kitten
kiwi
koala

Click the Mouse!
For more fun with the letter K, check out pbskids.org/lions/gryphonhouse.
Story: King Midas
Game: Theo's Puzzles (k)

·····Letter Kk·····

35

Ll

Lions and Lemons, Oh My!

Explore the taste of food that begins with the letter L, such as lemons, lettuce, lasagna, and lemonade.

My Left Hand

If your child is right-handed, ask him to use his left hand to perform everyday tasks, such as brushing his teeth or eating his cereal. Is it easier for him to use his right hand or his left hand? Remind your child that left is a word that begins with the letter L, which makes the /l/ sound.

Leona's Tongue Twister

Have fun saying this tongue twister three times fast.

Leona and Lionel like lemonade.

Looby Loo

Enjoy singing and acting out this song while emphasizing all the words that begin with the /l/ sound.

Looby Loo

Here we go looby loo,
Here we go looby light,
Here we go looby loo,
All on a Saturday night.
You put your right hand in.
You take your right hand out.
You give your hand a
shake, shake, shake,
And turn yourself about

Additional verses:

…You put your left hand in…
…You put your right foot in…
…You put your left foot in…
…You put your whole self in…

Note: If you are unfamiliar with this song or any other song in this book, use a search engine to find places on the web where you can hear it.

L Is for LION

What You Will Need
masking tape or chalk

What to Do

- With masking tape or chalk, make a large uppercase letter L and a large lowercase letter l side by side on the floor or sidewalk.
- Have your child roar loudly like an adult lion as he marches with big steps along the uppercase letter L, moving from top to bottom.
- Then have your child roar softly like a lion cub as he marches with little steps along the lowercase letter l.

More Ideas

Listening Walk

Take your child outside on a listening walk. Pause occasionally to stop and listen quietly. Ask, *What do you hear? What is making that sound? Do you hear anything else?* Write down the different sounds your child names and describes. As you listen for sounds, point out that the word listen begins with the letter L, which makes the /l/ sound.

Roar Like a Lion

Help your child practice listening for the /l/ sound at the beginning of familiar words. Say /l/ words such as *lollipop, lemon, lion,* and *lamp.* Add a challenge by saying some words that begin with /l/ and others that do not, such as *lamb, leaf, car,* and *light.* Ask your child to roar like a lion when he hears a word that begins with the /l/ sound.

Read *Lola at the Library* by Anna McQuinn, *Lucille Lost: A True Adventure* by Margaret George and Christopher J. Murphy, *The Three Little Pigs* by Paul Galdone, *Little Red Hen* by Byron Barton, *The Grouchy Ladybug* by Eric Carle, or *The Lion and the Mouse* by Bernadette Watts, emphasizing the /l/ sound as you read.

Click the Mouse!

For more fun with the letter L, check out pbskids.org/lions/gryphonhouse.

Stories:	The Lion and the Mouse
	The Little Red Hen
	The Three Little Pigs
Songs:	Look It Up
Video Clips:	I Love My Family

Ll

Letter L Vocabulary

lamb
lamp
lap
lasagna
leaf
leap
left
leg
lemon
lemonade
leopard
letter
lettuce
library
lime
lion
lips
little
lobster
log
lollipop
love
lunch

·····Letter Ll·····

Mm

M Alliteration

Say a few alliterative sentences that feature the /m/ sound of the letter M, and then ask your child to make up his own. For example:

I miss my mama.
The moon is made of mud.
Mice munch muffins.

Milk Tastes Like...

Drink a glass of milk and take turns describing how it tastes or looks.

Milk tastes like sunshine.
Milk looks like liquid chalk.

Try this with other foods that begin with the letter M, such as macaroni or melon.

Magazine Stories

Cut out three or more pictures from a magazine. Point out that the word magazine begins with the letter M, which makes the /m/ sound. Help your child use the three pictures to make up a story. For example, if the three pictures are of a rake, a house, and a tree, the story could be that a big wind storm blew twigs and leaves off the tree and into the yard of the house. The family living in the house had to use a rake to clean up the yard.

Sing an M

Enjoy singing this song, emphasizing all the words that begin with the letter M, which makes the /m/ sound.

Do You Know the Muffin Man?

Oh, do you know the muffin man,
The muffin man, the muffin man?
Oh, do you know the muffin man,
Who lives in Drury Lane?

Oh, yes, I know the muffin man,
The muffin man, the muffin man.
Oh, yes, I know the muffin man,
Who lives in Drury Lane.

Note: If you are unfamiliar with this song or any other song in this book, use a search engine to find places on the web where you can hear it.

L Is for LION

Matching Game

What You Will Need

picture cards of baby animals (calf, kitten, puppy, and so on) and corresponding animal mothers (cow, cat, dog, and so on) **Note:** You can purchase sets of picture cards with animal babies and mothers, or you can make your own set by cutting out pictures of animals and gluing or taping them to index cards. Magazines and catalogs are good places to find pictures. If you have access to a computer, search for pictures of animal babies and mothers and print them out.

What to Do

- Place the picture cards in front of your child.
- Ask your child to match pictures of baby animals with their mothers.
- Talk about the matches, noting that the words *match* and *mother* begin with the letter M, which makes the /m/ sound.
- Say, *Yes, that's the baby cat's mother. Do you know what a baby cat is called? It's called a kitten.*

More Ideas

Moon Cookies

Snack on moon cookies. Make your favorite sugar cookie recipe with your child, and then use circle- or crescent-shaped cookie cutters to make moon-shaped cookies, or shape the dough by hand. You can also nibble any round cookie, making the changing shapes of the moon by slowly eating half of a round moon cookie to make a half moon. Continue eating until you have a crescent moon!

Monkey See, Monkey Do

Tell your child to copy your actions. If you hop on one foot, she should hop on one foot. If you scratch your leg, she should scratch her leg. Then copy your child's action.

Read *Violet's Music* by Angela Johnson; *Miss Mary Mack* by Mary Ann Hoberman; *Moo Moo, Brown Cow* by Jakki Wood; or *I Miss You, Stinky Face* by Lisa McCourt, emphasizing the /m/ sound as you read.

Click the Mouse!
For more fun with the letter M, check out pbskids.org/lions/gryphonhouse.

Stories:	The Ants and the Grasshopper
	Violet's Music
Song:	Miniscule
Game:	Monkey Match

Mm

Letter M Vocabulary

macaroni
magazine
mama
map
mask
match
melon
mice
milk
mom
monkey
moon
moose
mop
mother
mouse
muffin
mud
mug
munch
music

Nn

Eating N

Enjoy a snack or meal of foods that begin with the letter N, such as nuts, noodles, and nachos.

Practice the Sound

Tell your child that the letter N makes the /n/ sound. Say a word beginning with /n/, such as *night*, emphasizing the beginning /n/ sound: *nnnight*. Have your child repeat the /n/ sound with you. Repeat with other words that begin with the /n/ sound, such as *nut, nest, noise,* and *nachos.*

Rub Noses

Rub noses with your child. Say the word nose, emphasizing the /n/ sound.

Neighborhood Pictures

Provide paper and art materials, such as crayons, markers, scissors, tissue paper, glue, glitter, construction paper, paint, and paintbrushes, and suggest that your child create a real or imaginary picture of your neighborhood.
Note: Your child can use his picture as a guide when creating his neighborhood from blocks. (See "Our Neighborhood" on the next page.)

Read Night in the Country by Cynthia Rylant, Nutmeg and Barley: A Budding Friendship by Janie Bynum, Not Norman by Kelly Bennett, or Little Nino's Pizzeria by Karen Barbour, emphasizing the /n/ sound as you read.

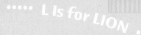

Our Neighborhood

What You Will Need

building blocks

labels

pencils

small plastic figures

What to Do

- Suggest that your child use blocks and other materials to build a neighborhood.
- Explain that a neighborhood, a word that begins with the letter N, is where you live. Your home, the houses, stores, schools, and parks nearby are all part of a neighborhood.
- Talk to your child about the things he sees as he walks in his neighborhood.
  Note: You may want to look at books about neighborhoods, such as *Knuffle Bunny* by Mo Willems and *Jonathan and His Mommy* by Irene Smalls.
- Suggest that your child build a make-believe neighborhood out of blocks, with buildings, sidewalks, and parks. Help label his structures. Add small plastic figures that can be moved around the neighborhood.

More Ideas

Number Hop

Create a set of numbers cards from 1 to 10 (or 1 to 5) with dots corresponding to the numbers. Tape the cards to the floor in numerical order. Explain that each card has a number, a word that begins with the letter N, and dots that show how many. The 1 card has one dot; the 2 card has two dots, and so on. Have your child count forward as he hops or walks down the number path. If he is ready, ask him to hop and count backward!

Nut Sort

Place an assortment of nuts (in their shells or shelled) in a bowl. Suggest that your child sort the nuts. As you talk with him about the nuts, emphasize that the word *nuts* begins with the letter N, which makes the /n/ sound.

Nn

Letter N
Vocabulary

nachos
nail
nap
neck
neighbor
neighborhood
nest
net
newspaper
night
no
noise
noodles
nose
number
nuts

Click the Mouse!

For more fun with the letter N, check out pbskids.org/lions/gryphonhouse.

Story: **Night in the Country**

Video Clips: **Cliff Hanger and the Nightingales**

Gawain's Word: night

Words Beginning with n

······Letter Nn······

41

Oo

Eat an O

Enjoy a meal or snack of round (like the letter O) food. Suggestions of food to serve include apples or oranges sliced horizontally; cereal that has a round shape; an English muffin pizza; and carrot slices.

Walk an O

Draw the outline of the letter O on the floor with tape or chalk. Show your child how to walk along the round line.

Find an O

Challenge your child to find things that are round like the shape of the letter O. Objects that your child might find are a clock with a round face, a round plate, a round pan, or a round block.

Sing About Opposites

Emphasize the short sound of the letter O in the words *opposites* and *stop* as you sing this song to the tune of "Do You Know the Muffin Man?" After your child is familiar with the short sound of O, sing the sing again and listen for the long sound of the letter O in words like *oh, go, no, low,* and *slow.*

The Opposite Song

Oh, do you know some opposites, some opposites,
*   some opposites?*
Oh, do you know some opposites? Opposites are fun.

If I say stop, then you say go.
If I say yes, then you say no.
If I say fast, then you say slow. Oh, opposites are fun.

If I say low, then you say high.
If I say hi, then you say bye.
If I say wet, then you say dry. Oh, opposites are fun.

Decorate Letter O

What You Will Need

crayons

cutout pictures of round objects shaped like an O (button, clock, moon, sun, wheel, and so on) **Note:** Magazines and catalogs are good places to find pictures. If you have access to a computer, search for the pictures you need and print them out.

glue
hole punch
large cutout of the letter O
markers
paper
scissors
small round objects for gluing

Oo

What to Do

- Talk with your child about the shape of the letter O. Say, *The letter O is round like a circle, a cookie, or the moon. Let's look for other things that are round.* (buttons, wheels, and so on)
- Have your child decorate a large uppercase letter O with round shapes, including cutout circles of paper and paper circles from a hole punch.
- As your child works, talk with her about the name and the shape of the letter and the round objects on the letter.

Another Idea

Opposites

Play an opposite game. Say, *Watch what I do. Instead of doing what I do, I want you to do the opposite.* Nod your head yes as you say, *I'm nodding my head yes. Now you do the opposite.* Ask, *What are you doing? You are shaking your head no.* Next, sit down as you say, *I'm sitting down. Now you do the opposite.* Ask, *What are you doing? You are standing up.*

**Letter O
Vocabulary**

oak
oatmeal
oboe
ocean
octopus
odd
okra
olive
omelet
on
opposite
orange
otter
over

Read *The Fox and the Crow* by Susan Ring, *Where Butterflies Grow* by Joanne Ryder, or *Growing Colors* by Bruce McMillan, emphasizing the short or long sound of the letter O as you read.

Click the Mouse!
For more fun with the letter O, check out pbskids.org/lions/gryphonhouse.

Story:	Otter's Picnic
Songs:	Double o, oo
	Home Is Where Long o Is
	If You Can Read op
Video Clips:	Opposite Bunny: fast/slow
	Vowel Boot Camp: not/note
Games:	Dub Cubs
	Hopposites

Pp

Practice the Sound

Tell your child that the letter P makes the /p/ sound. Say a word beginning with /p/, such as puppy, emphasizing the beginning /p/ sound: *pppuppy*. Have your child repeat the /p/ sound with you. Repeat with other words that begin with the /p/ sound, such as *popcorn, paper, peas,* and *pig.*

Feel the P

Select a word that begins with the letter P, such as *pig* or *popcorn.* Ask your child to place his hand in front of his mouth and say the word. Ask. *Did you feel air on your hand?* Say, *When you make the /p/ sound, you push air out of your mouth. Let's say* pig *again. Listen for the /p/ sound.*

Purple and Pink, Oh My!

Provide purple and pink (two colors that begin with the letter P) art materials (paper, markers, crayons, paint and paintbrushes, glitter, pompoms, and any other art material) and suggest that your child create purple-and-pink artwork.

Letter P Puzzle

Make a letter P puzzle by gluing pictures of objects that begin with the letter P, such as pigs, pails, peacocks, pencils, or paint on pieces of cardboard. Cut the pictures into two or more pieces and challenge your child to put the puzzle back together. Point out that the objects and the word *puzzle* begin with the letter P, which makes the /p/ sound.

Note: Magazines and catalogs are good places to find pictures of objects. If you have access to a computer, search for objects that begin with the letter P and print them out.

The Pattern of P

What You Will Need

objects or pictures of objects that begin with the letter P (pan, pancake, panther, peach, peacock, peanuts, pear, pencil, peppermint, pig, popcorn, pretzel, or puppy)

What to Do

- Search for objects or pictures of objects that begin with the letter P. (Magazines and catalogs are good places to find pictures of objects. If you have access to a computer, search for objects that begin with the letter P and print them out.)
  Note: You will need multiple sets of each object, or pictures of each object, to make patterns.
- Talk with your child about patterns (a word that begins with the letter P). Decide which pattern you want to use. You can begin with a simple alternating pattern (ABABAB) and then progress to more complicated patterns, such as ABCABCABC, AABBAABBAABBA. The possibilities are endless. Once you decide which pattern you are using, help your child create it with the objects or pictures.
- Encourage your child to make up her own patterns.

More Ideas

Pink and Purple

Provide a very large pink uppercase P and lowercase p. Your child can use purple markers and crayons to decorate the letters with polka dots, stripes, squiggles, zigzags, and curly and wiggly lines. Encourage her to talk about the designs she is making.

Letter P Poster

Suggest that your child search through catalogs and magazines to find pictures of things that begin with the letter P, and then cut out the pictures and glue them onto poster board or paper to make a "Letter P Poster."

Read *Popcorn* by Frank Asch, *What Pete Ate from A to Z* by Maira Kalman, *Pete's a Pizza* by William Steig, or *Pigs Aplenty, Pigs Galore!* by David McPhail, emphasizing the /p/ sound as you read.

Click the Mouse!
For more fun with the letter P, check out
pbskids.org/lions/gryphonhouse.
Stories: Piggy's Pictures
          The Three-Legged Pot
          Worm Paints
Song: Sloppy Pop
Video Clip: Play with Words: pants/ants

Pp

·····Letter Pp·····

Qq

Letter Pals

Write *queen,* or any other word that begins with the letter Q on a piece of paper. Explain that the letter Q has a letter pal, the letter U. The letter Q is almost never seen without the letter U next to it. Say, *Together they make the /kw/ sound, like in the word* queen. Help your child recognize the /kw/ sound in the beginning of familiar words such as *queen, question,* and *quilt.*

Quiet Words

How quietly can you say a word and still be heard? Take turns saying words very quietly to determine just how quietly you can say a word and still be understood.

Quick as a Q

Draw the outline of the uppercase letter Q on the floor with tape or chalk. Show your child how to walk quickly along the round line and the short, straight line.

Quacking Away

Sing "Five Little Ducks" to learn about the sound /kw/ that the letter pals of Q and U make. What fun!
Note: On songsforteaching.com, kiddiddles.com, YouTube.com, and many other websites, you can hear this song and many others. If you don't know the tune, you can chant the song instead of singing it.

That's Quite a Quilt!

What You Will Need

box filled with a variety of small materials that can be
    glued or attached to poster board (buttons,
    cotton balls, feathers, ribbons, sequins, stickers,
    tissue paper, yarn, and so on)

crayons   glue

markers   poster board

squares of construction paper   tape

What to Do

- Suggest that your child create quilt squares by decorating squares of construction paper.
- After your child has completed enough squares, glue the decorated squares onto a piece of poster board. (It may take a few days for your child to decorate enough construction paper squares to fill the poster board.)
- Talk with your child about her quilt, emphasizing the /kw/ sound at the beginning of the word *quilt*.

More Ideas

Trace It!

Trace the letter Q on your child's back. Can she identify the letter? Try this with other letters. Ask your child to trace a letter onto your back. Can you identify the letter?

It's in the Air!

Help your child recognize and begin to "write" the letter Q. While your child is watching you, trace in the air the shape of the uppercase letter Q. Make the circle first, continuing until the circle is closed. Add a slanted line to make the "tail."

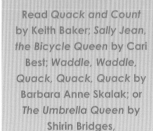

Read *Quack and Count* by Keith Baker; *Sally Jean, the Bicycle Queen* by Cari Best; *Waddle, Waddle, Quack, Quack, Quack* by Barbara Anne Skalak; or *The Umbrella Queen* by Shirin Bridges, emphasizing the /kw/ sound as you read.

Click the Mouse!
For more fun with the letter Q, check out
pbskids.org/lions/gryphonhouse.
Song: Q without U
Poem: Quack, Quack!
Video Clip: Joy Learno: Queen Bee

Qq

Letter Q Vocabulary

quack
quail
quarrel
quart
quarter
queen
question
question mark
quick
quiet
quilt

Rr

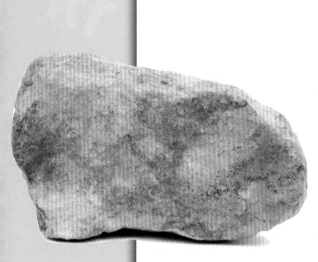

Decorate an R

Draw the outline of a large uppercase R on a piece of paper. Suggest that your child trace the outline of the letter with a rainbow pencil or markers or crayons in rainbow colors.

Robin Begins with R

Draw the outline of the letter R on the floor with tape or chalk. Have your child pretend to be a robin (a word that begins with the letter R) looking for worms as he pecks the curved and straight lines of the letter R.

Red Is Everywhere

Provide red art materials (paper, pompoms, markers, crayons, chalk, glitter, tape, tissue paper, stickers, buttons, beads, and any other red material). As your child creates a red art project, explain that the color red begins with the letter R, which makes the /r/ sound. Say, red, emphasizing the beginning /r/ sound: rrred.

Read a Book

Sing the following to the tune of "Row, Row, Row Your Boat." Emphasize the /r/ sound in the song.

Read, Read, Read a Book
Read, read, read a book
Every single day.
Merrily, merrily, merrily, merrily
Every single day.

Read *A Rainbow All Around Me* by Sandra L. Pinkney; *Sheila Rae, the Brave* by Kevin Henkes; *Roller Coaster* by Marla Frazee; or *The Little Red Hen* by Paul Galdone, emphasizing the /r/ sound as you read.

Rhyming Game

What You Will Need

no materials needed

What to Do

- Explain that when two words rhyme, they have the same ending sound. Point out that the word *rhyme* begins with the /r/ sound.
- Ask your child to listen carefully as you say two words.
- Say, *If the two words rhyme, quack like a duck—duck, tuck. Do they rhyme? Yes! Quack!*
- Repeat with more rhyming words, such as rock/sock, red/bed, ride/tide, log/frog, fish/dish, fox/box, cake/rake/ ball/wall, and ring/swing.
- Change the rhyming response from a quack to a clap or to a jump.
- Alternate with pairs of words that don't rhyme, such as cat/dog, car/plane, doll/house, and ball/can. Make up a response to words that don't rhyme, such as a raspberry, a boo, or thumbs-down.

More Ideas

Rhyming Pairs

Show your child a number of pictures, some that form rhyming pairs and other that do not. Ask your child to find the pairs that rhyme. **Note:** Magazines and catalogs are good places to find pictures of objects. If you have access to a computer, search for pictures of pairs that rhyme and others that do not rhyme and print them out.

Sounds Like the Letter R

Play a sound game to help your child hear and recognize the /r/ sound at the beginning of familiar words. Say the word *rocket* slowly, emphasizing the initial /r/ sound. Ask, *What sound do you hear at the beginning of the word rrrocket?* Display a ring along with other small items that begin with the /r/ sound, such as a ruler, rope, rock, and a few items that do not begin with the /r/ sound, such as a ball, comb, and block. Name each item. Ask your child to point to the things that begin with the /r/ sound. Hold up the rock and ask, *Does the word rock begin with the same sound as the word ring?* Say, *r-ing, r-ock. Yes, the word rock begins with the /r/ sound.* Suggest that your child pick up an object, name it, and say whether it begins with the /r/ sound.

Rr

Letter R Vocabulary

rabbit
raccoon
rain
rainbow
raisins
rake
raspberry
rat
read
red
refrigerator
rhinoceros
rhyme
rice
ring
river
robin
rock
rocket
rooster
round
rug
ruler

Click the Mouse!
For more fun with the letter R, check out pbskids.org/lions/gryphonhouse.

Stories:	The Little Red Hen
	Roller Coaster
Songs:	Read a Book Today!
	Rocket-Doodle-Doo
Video Clips:	Cliff Hanger, the River, and the Rain
	Fred: rooster
Word Morph:	rock-robin-rowboat

•••••Letter Rr •••••

49

Ss

Silver S
Tear foil or other silver papers into small pieces. Draw a large letter S on a sheet of paper. Invite your child to decorate the large S letter with the torn pieces of silver paper and star stickers. Ask your child to describe the silvery letter S that sparkles with stars. Tell your child that *silvery, stars,* and *stickers* are words that begin with the letter S, which makes the /s/ sound.

Twist Your Tongue Around the Letter S
Say the following sentence slowly: *Silvery stars sparkle in the sky.* Challenge your child to repeat the sentence three times fast.

The Last Sound You Hear
Talk about the /s/ sound that you hear at the end of plural words, such as stars, bears, and stickers. Hold up a single cutout star. Ask, *How many stars do I have in my hand? Yes, I have one star.* Have your child repeat the word *star* with you. Hold up two cutout stars. Ask, *How many stars do I have now? I have two stars.* Ask your child to say the word *stars* with you, stretching the final /s/ sound: *starsssss.* Ask, *What sound do you hear at the end of the word stars?* Explain that sometimes when we hear the /s/ sound at the end of a word, it means that there is more than one. Say, *One star, two stars.*

See the Sea
Enjoy all the /s/ sounds in the following song.

A Sailor Went to Sea Sea Sea
A sailor went to sea sea sea
To see what he could see see see.
But all that he could see see see
Was the bottom of the deep blue sea sea sea!

Note: If you are unfamiliar with this song or any other song in this book, use a search engine to find places on the web where you can hear it.

Star Paintings

What You Will Need

construction paper
star-shaped sponges and/or cookie cutters
paint
tray
writing materials

What to Do

- Invite your child to dip star-shaped sponges or cookie cutters into a tray of paint to make star-shaped prints or patterns on paper.
- Emphasize that the word *star* begins with the letter S, which makes the /s/ sound.
- Ask your child questions that encourage her to talk about her picture.

More Ideas

Wish upon a Star

Cut out a star shape. Teach your child the following rhyme:

Star light, star bright,   *I wish I may, I wish I might*
First star I see tonight.   *Have this wish I wish tonight.*

Tell your child that she can dictate her wish on one side of the star and decorate the other side.

Star and Moon Patterns

Cut out star and moon (circles) shapes from construction paper. Show your child the shapes. Ask her to describe each shape. Say, *The round circle is the moon. This shape is a star.* Ask, *How many points does the star have?* Create a simple pattern with the moon and star shapes: star, star, moon; star, star.... Ask, *What should come next, a star or a moon?* Invite your child to make her own pattern with the shapes.

Read *Sylvie & True* by David McPhail, *Silly Sally* by Audrey Wood, or one of the versions of the story of *Stone Soup* by Ann McGovern, Marcia Brown, and many other authors, emphasizing the /s/ sound as you read.

Click the Mouse!
For more fun with the letter S, check out pbskids.org/lions/gryphonhouse.

Stories:	A Shower of Stars
	Stone Soup
Song:	Without an s
Poem:	Little Seeds
Video Clips:	Play with Words: snail/nail
Tongue Twister:	This Is the Sixth Sister

Letter S Vocabulary

sad
salad
salmon
sand
sandwich
sauce
sea
see
seed
seesaw
seven
sew
silver
sink
sister
six
sky
soap
sock
soup
spin
star
sun

····· Letter Ss ·····

Tt

What Does Your Tongue Taste?

Explore a variety of foods that begin with the letter T, which makes the /t/ sound. Expand this /t/ sound experience by tasting the foods with the tip of your tongue. Foods that you might want to consider are tomatoes, tacos, tamales, and turkey.

Two Fingers Together for T

Show your child how to use your two index fingers to make a lowercase t and an uppercase T. Ask your child to do the same.

Note: If you are unfamiliar with this song or any other song in this book, use a search engine to find places on the web where you can hear it.

Teddy Bear Sounds

Emphasize all the /t/ sounds in this chant. Add the actions for more fun!

Teddy Bear, Teddy Bear
*Teddy bear, teddy bear,
Turn around.* (Turn around.)
*Teddy bear, teddy bear,
Touch the ground.*
    (Touch the ground.)

*Teddy bear, teddy bear,
Tie your shoe.*
    (Pretend to tie your shoe.)
*Teddy bear, teddy bear,
Show me two.*
    (Hold up two fingers.)

*Teddy bear, teddy bear,
Turn off the light.* (Pretend to turn off a light.)
*Teddy bear, teddy bear,
Say, "Sleep tight"!*
    (Pretend to sleep.)

Twinkle the Night Away

Emphasize the /t/ sound as you sing this song.

Twinkle, Twinkle, Little Star
Twinkle, twinkle, little star,
    (Open and close your fingers as you say each word.)
How I wonder what you are.
    (Look up as you sing.)
Up above the world so high,
    (Reach up to the sky.)
Like a diamond in the sky.
    (Make a diamond shape with your hands.)
Twinkle, twinkle, little star,
    (Open and close your fingers as you say each word.)
How I wonder what you are.
    (Look up as you sing.)

I Hear the Sound

What You Will Need

toy animals or pictures of animals that begin with the /t/ sound (turtle, tiger, turkey) and others that do not begin with the /t/ sound

actual foods, or pictures of foods that begin with the /t/ sound (tomato, tea, tortilla, taco) and others that do not begin with the /t/ sound

actual instruments, or pictures of instruments that begin with the /t/ sound (tambourine, tuba, triangle) and others that do not begin with the /t/ sound

Note: Magazines and catalogs are good places to find pictures of objects. If you have access to a computer, search for the pictures you need and print them out.

What to Do

- Play a guessing game using objects or pictures that belong to three categories: animals, foods, and instruments. Tell your child to listen to your clues.
- Show your child pictures of animals or plastic animals, including a turtle. Say, *I'm thinking of an animal that starts with the /t/ sound. The animal has a hard shell. Can you guess what it is? What is another animal that begins with the /t/ sound?* (tiger)
- Show your child musical instruments or pictures of instruments, including a tambourine. Say, *I'm thinking of a musical instrument that you shake. It begins with the /t/ sound.* Ask, *Can you guess what it is? What is another musical instrument that begins with the /t/ sound?* (tuba)
- Display different foods or pictures of foods, including a tomato. Say, *I'm thinking of a food that you eat. It's red, round, and juicy and begins with the /t/ sound.* Ask, *Can you guess what it is? What is another food that begins with the /t/ sound?* (taco)

Another Idea

Toe Touches

Challenge your child to use his toe to touch objects in the room. For example, tell him to touch his toe to the table, to the wall, or to the chair. Point out that the words *toe, touch,* and *table* all begin with the letter T, which makes the /t/ sound.

Read *Treasure* by Suzanne Bloom, *Sylvie & True* by David McPhail, *A Birthday Basket for Tía* by Pat Mora, *Mrs. Katz and Tush* by Patricia Polacco, or *Terrific* by Jon Agee, emphasizing the /t/ sound as you read.

Click the Mouse!

For more fun with the letter T, check out **pbskids.org/lions/gryphonhouse.**
Story: **Tabby Cat at Night**
Video Clips: **Play with Words: train/rain**

Tt

Letter T Vocabulary

table
tacos
tamales
tambourine
teddy bear
tent
tiger
time
toe
tomato
tongue
top
touch
toy
train
transportation
tuba
turkey
turtle
two

Uu

Upside Down Art

Tape a piece of paper underneath a table. Provide art materials—paper, markers, and crayons—so your child can create "upside down" art.

I Hear a U

Say words that begin with the short sound /u/ to help your child begin to recognize the sound of the letter U. Start with the words *up, uncle,* and *umbrella*. When your child is familiar with the short /u/ sound, introduce words with the long sound of the letter U in words such as *ukulele, unicorn,* and *universe*.

Walk Along a U

Draw the outline of the letter U on the floor with tape or chalk. Show your child how to walk along the straight and curvy parts of the line.

Underline the Letters

Give your child a marker and a page from a toy catalog or a magazine with large type. Ask her to underline all the Us that she finds on the page.

The Shape of U

What You Will Need

clay, playdough, or pipe cleaners

index cards

markers

What to Do

- Write an uppercase U and a lowercase u on an index card.
- Talk with your child about the shapes of the uppercase U and lowercase u.
- Suggest that your child use clay, playdough, or pipe cleaners to make an uppercase U and lowercase u.

More Ideas

Umbrella Art

Help your child cut out umbrella shapes and then use art materials to decorate them. Hang the completed umbrella-shaped pictures in a window.

My Unicorn

Help your child create a story about a unicorn that lives under a big umbrella. Challenge her to use as many words as she can that begin with the letter U. Write her story on paper so she understands that words and stories can be written.

Uu

Read *Knuffle Bunny* by Mo Willems, *The Umbrella* by Jan Brett, *One Duck Stuck* by Phyllis Root, or *Hug* by Jez Alborough, emphasizing the /u/ sound as you read.

Click the Mouse!

For more fun with the letter U, check out pbskids.org/lions/gryphonhouse.

Story: The Emperor's New Clothes

Songs: If You Can Read: ug
Upper and Lowercase

Game: Dub Cubs

•••••Letter Uu ••••••

Vv

Eat Your Vs!

Eat vegetables, such as carrots, celery, cucumbers, and green peppers. As you eat, talk about the variety of foods that are vegetables, a word that begins with the letter V, which makes the /v/ sound.

Flowers in a Vase

Arrange an assortment of flowers in a vase. Talk about the colors of the flowers in the vase, a word that begins with the letter V, which makes the /v/ sound.

Walk Along a V

Draw the outline of the letter V on the floor with tape or chalk. Show your child how to walk down one line and up the other line. Challenge your child to hop, tiptoe, or jump along the lines of the letter.

Violet Collage

Provide an assortment of violet art materials, such as construction paper, stickers, crayons, markers, paints and brushes, and encourage your child to use the art materials to make a Violet Collage.

Read *Violet's Music* by Angela Johnson or *Zin! Zin! Zin! A Violin!* by Lloyd Moss, or *The Very Busy Spider*, *The Very Clumsy Click Beetle*, *The Very Lonely Firefly*, or *The Very Quiet Cricket* by Eric Carle, emphasizing the /v/ sound as you read.

Valentines!

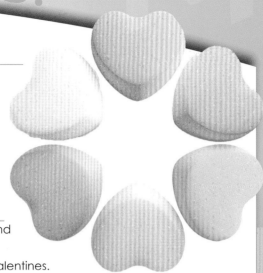

What You Will Need
crayons
glue or tape
markers
paper
scissors
stickers

What to Do
- Any day is a great day to let your friends and family know how you feel about them!
- Use art materials to help your child make valentines.
- Give or send them to friends and family members.

More Ideas

Vinegar Volcano
Create a "volcano" by covering the outside of a small, empty soda bottle with clay or playdough. Keep the hole of the soda bottle clear of clay or playdough. Place the soda bottle volcano in a baking pan. Fill the soda bottle halfway with warm water. Add two tablespoons of baking soda into the bottle, and then add half a cup of vinegar to make the volcano "erupt."
Note: This can be messy, but also a lot of fun!

Change That Vowel!
Use simple, three-letter words to play this change-the-vowel game. Write a word like *cat* on paper. Explain that by changing one letter—the vowel in the middle— you can make a new word. For example, *cat* can change to *cot* or *cut*; *tan* can change to *ten* or *tin*; *pat* can change to *pet, pit,* or *pat.*

Click the Mouse!
For more fun with the letter V, check out pbskids.org/lions/gryphonhouse.
Story:	The Hungry Coat
Songs:	Can't Make a Word without a Vowel
	Very Loud, Very Big, Very Metal
Video Clips:	Cliff Hanger and the Very Powerful Vacuum Cleaner
	Dinos Read: veterinarian
	Vegetables, Yum!

Letter V Vocabulary
vacuum cleaner
valentine
van
vanilla
vase
vegetable
very
vest
veterinarian
vine
vinegar
violet
violin
viper
volcano
vote
vowel
vulture

Ww

Walk Like a Wolf

Use tape or chalk to make the letter W on the floor or sidewalk. Suggest that your child walk, slink, or creep like a wolf along the lines of the letter W, beginning at the starting point on the upper left and following the lines of the letter. Point out that the words *walk* and *wolf* begin with the letter W, which makes the /w/ sound.

Waffles and Watermelon

Eat waffles and watermelon for breakfast, or anytime during the day! Top the waffles with walnuts to add another delicious W food to the meal.

Wiggle Like a Worm

Say the following poem. Encourage your child to wiggle like a worm.

Wiggle, Wiggle

Wiggle, wiggle little worm,
How I like to watch you squirm!
Down your hole you quickly go
Safely hiding from your foe.

Wiggle, wiggle little worm,
How I like to watch you squirm!
Down your hole you quickly run
Safely hiding from the sun.

Which Word Is Longer?

Say, *I am going to say the names of two animals. Listen carefully, then tell me which word is longer.* Before each pair of words, ask your child, *Which of these words is longer?* Slowly say the following pairs of words: wand/wallpaper, wall/watermelon, wink/woodpecker, worm/wonderful, wood/wallaby, wolf/woodchuck. Pause after saying each pair of words. To show your child the length of each word, write each pair of words, one directly below the other.

Walk Like This

What You Will Need

no materials needed

What to Do

- Sing this song about different ways of walking, a word that begins with the letter W.
- Practice different ways of walking or moving, such as taking crisscross steps, hopping, taking baby steps, tiptoeing, and so on.
- Sing the following song to the tune of "Here We Go 'Round the Mulberry Bush."
- Add verses by replacing the words in the last line with different steps.
- Sing the different verses and move as described in each verse.

This Is the Way the Children Walk

This is the way the children walk,
The children walk,
The children walk.
This is the way the children walk,
Hop, hop, hop.

Other verses (Substitute one of the following for the fifth line):

Skip, skip, skip
Step, step, step
Baby step, baby step, baby step
Tiptoe, tiptoe, tiptoe

More Ideas

Find That W!

Help your child find the letter W in signs, labels, and book titles around the room or around your neighborhood.

I Wish I Were ...

Ask your child to finish this sentence: "I wish I were..." Talk about wishes, a word that begins with the letter W, which makes the /w/ sound.

Read *Wonderful Worms* by Linda Glaser, *I Wanna Iguana* by Karen Kaufman, *Worried* by Kevin Henkes, *The Wednesday Surprise* by Eve Bunting, or *Winter Is the Warmest Season* by Lauren Stringer, emphasizing the /w/ sound as you read.

For more fun with the letter W, check out pbskids.org/lions/gryphonhouse.

Stories:	Wonderful Worms
	Worm Watches
Song:	W Trouble
Video Clips:	Fred: wiggle
	Lions Wiggling

Ww

Letter W Vocabulary

waffle
wagon
walk
wall
walnut
walrus
wand
watch
water
watermelon
weasel
wiggle
wing
wink
wish
wolf
wonderful
wood
woodchuck
woodpecker
wool
word
worm

Xx

Eat an X

Show your child how to cross two pretzel sticks, sticks of cheese, or celery or carrot sticks to make an X. Challenge your child to make his own Xs and then eat them!

Make an X

Have your child use his body to make the letter X. One way is to cross one pointer finger over the other. Additional ways include raising his arms and crossing one over the other or lying on the floor, raising his legs into the air, and crossing one over the other.

Box Sculpture

Give your child a few boxes in a variety of shapes and sizes. Challenge him to use tape, glue, paint, and paintbrushes to make a box sculpture. Point out that the word box ends with /ks/, the sound of the letter X.

Hunt for X

Sing the following, emphasizing the /ks/ sound of the letter X at the end of the words fox and box.

A-Hunting We Will Go

A hunting we will go,
A hunting we will go!
We'll catch a little fox
And put him in a box
And then we'll let him go!

Note: If you are unfamiliar with this song or any other song in this book, use a search engine to find places on the web where you can hear it.

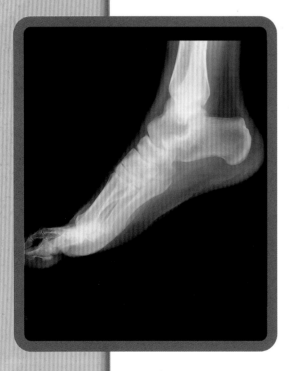

The Last Sound

What You Will Need

box

pictures of a fox, an ox, and the number six

> **Note:** Magazines and catalogs are good places to find pictures of objects. If you have access to a computer, search for the pictures that you need and print them out.

What to Do

- Play a listening game to help your child hear and recognize the /ks/ sound that the letter X makes at the end of words.
- Show your child a box. Ask, *What is this? Let's say the word together:* box. *Did you hear the /ks/ sound at the end of the word? Let's say it again:* box.
- Repeat the process with the words *fox, six,* and *ox*. Show your child pictures of a fox, the number six, and an ox.

More Ideas

Sounds Like a Xylophone

Fill glasses with different amounts of water and gently tap them with a wooden spoon to make your own "xylophone."

Trace an X

While your child is watching, write an uppercase X on paper. Draw a rectangular box on another sheet of paper. Tell your child that to make an X, he needs to draw two slanted lines in the box. He should start at the upper left corner and draw a slanted line to the lower right corner. Then make a second slanted line from the upper right corner to the lower left. The two lines cross in the middle.

Read *Pandora's Box* by Jean Marzollo, *The Fox and the Crow* by Susan Ring, or *I'll Fix Anthony* by Judith Viorst, emphasizing the /ks/ sound as you read.

Click the Mouse!

For more fun with the letter X, check out pbskids.org/lions/gryphonhouse.

Poem: X

Video Clip: Fred Says: fix/six

Xx

Letter X Vocabulary

X in the beginning of a word:
x-ray
xylophone

X at the end of a word:
fax
fix
fox
mix
ox
sax
six
wax

X in the middle of a word:
next
saxophone
taxi

·····Letter Xx ·····

Yy

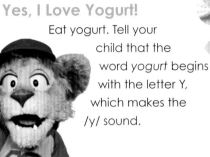

Yes, I Love Yogurt!

Eat yogurt. Tell your child that the word *yogurt* begins with the letter Y, which makes the /y/ sound.

Y Alliteration

Try to say one of the following sentences three times fast:

Yaks are yucky!
Yes, yellow yams taste yummy!

Yellow Y

Draw a large letter Y on paper. Give your child yellow crayons, markers, paint, or yarn, and other art materials. Let your child paint the letter yellow or decorate it with yellow circles, stripes, stars, yarn, and wiggly lines.

Yellow Yarn Pictures

Ask your child to draw a picture. Give her yellow yarn to glue on her picture to highlight certain parts.

Read *Yo! Yes?* by Chris Raschka, *I Love You Because You're You* by Liz Baker, *If You're Happy and You Know It* by Jane Cabrera, or *Bein' with You This Way* by W. Nikola-Lisa, emphasizing the /y/ sound as you read.

The Three Ys

What You Will Need

markers

paper or index cards

What to Do

- Write three words beginning with the letter Y on a piece of paper or an index card. Begin with words that are familiar to your child, such as *yes, yummy,* and *you.*
- Point to each word and say it aloud. Ask your child to repeat the words with you.
- Ask your child to identify the first letter in the words *yes, yummy,* and *you.*
- Repeat the words. Ask, *Can you hear the /y/ sound at the beginning of each word? What are other words that begin with the /y/ sound?* (yak, yucky, yarn, yellow, yam)

More Ideas

Is This Longer Than a Yard or Shorter Than a Yard?

Show your child a yardstick and challenge her to find things that are longer than a yard or shorter than a yard. Remind her that the word *yard* begins with the letter Y, which makes the /y/ sound.

Yoga

Yoga can help children relax and develop flexibility and coordination. A good way to begin is to sit in a comfortable position, close your eyes, and breathe in and out to the count of eight. After your child has mastered the breathing, try a simple position such as child's pose or downward-facing dog. If you are unfamiliar with yoga, there are a number of books (such as *Yoga Games for Children* by Danielle Bersma), DVDs (such as Yoga Kids: For Ages 3–6), and websites (such as yogakids.com) that will provide the information you need.

Click the Mouse!

For more fun with the letter Y, check out pbskids.org/lions/gryphonhouse.

Stories:	Oh, Yes, It Can!
	Yo! Yes?
Poem:	Yellow
Video Clip:	Opposite Bunny: yucky/yummy

Yy

Letter Y Vocabulary

yak
yam
yard
yarn
yawn
year
yellow
yellow beans
yellow squash
yes
yoga
yogurt
you
young
your
yoyo
yucky
yummy

..... Letter Yy .....

Zz

Buzzzzing Bees

Explain that the /z/ sound of Z is a lot like the sound of buzzing bees. Pretend to be bees, making the /z/ sound as you zip around the room. Emphasize the /z/ sound in words such as zzzap, zzzonk, zzzing, and zzzip.

Zesty Ziti

Cook ziti and serve it to your child with a zesty (spicy) tomato sauce. Explain that the pasta your child is eating is called ziti and that it has a zesty (spicy) sauce on it, so your child is eating two foods that begin with the letter Z, which makes the /z/ sound.

Zebra Pictures

Give your child white paper and black crayons or markers. Suggest that he make a picture of a black-and-white zebra or a design with black-and-white stripes.

Zoom to the Moon!

Explain that the letter Z makes the /z/ sound. Emphasize this sound as you say the following poem.

Zoom, Zoom, Zoom

*Zoom, zoom, zoom (Rub
   hands upward.)
I'm going to the moon.
   (Zoom hands up.)
If you want to take a trip,
Climb aboard my rocket
   ship. (Climb an
   imaginary ladder.)
Zoom, zoom, zoom, (Rub
   hands upward.)
I'm going to the moon.
   (Zoom hands up.)*

Zigzag Dance

What You Will Need
No materials neeed

What to Do
- Use tape or chalk to draw a large letter Z on the floor or sidewalk.
- Beginning at the top left, walk along the zigzag line.
- As you walk, encourage your child to shout words that begin with the letter Z (*zipper, zucchini, zoom, zoo, zebra*) as he moves along the letter Z.

More Ideas

Animal Cracker Zoo
Give your child cream cheese, a graham cracker, and a few animal crackers to make an Animal Cracker Zoo as a snack. He can spread the cream cheese thickly on a graham cracker, then stand the animal crackers upright using the graham cracker as a platform. Encourage your child to say the names of the animals in his "zoo."

Sing About the Alphabet
Because we have reached the last letter of the alphabet, it's a **perfect** time to play the "Where Has the Alphabet Gone?" game! Hide a set of alphabet blocks or magnetic letters around the room. Sing the following to the tune of "Oh, Where, Oh, Where, Has My Little Dog Gone?" and then search for the letters of the alphabet.

Where Has the Alphabet Gone?
Oh, where, oh, where, has the alphabet gone?
Oh, where, oh, where, can it be?
With 26 letters from A to Z,
Oh, where, oh, where, can it be?

Read *Zin! Zin! Zin! A Violin!* by Lloyd Moss, *Mama Zooms* by Jane Cowen-Fletcher, *Ziggy Piggy and the Three Little Pigs* by Frank Asch, or *Abiyoyo* by Pete Seeger (which features the recurring phrase "Zoop! Zoop!"), emphasizing the /z/ sound as you read the story.

Click the Mouse!
For more fun with the letter Z, check out
pbskids.org/lions/gryphonhouse.
Song: Library A to Z
Video Clips: Cliff Hanger and the Sneezing Zebu
Fred Says: zipper

Zz

Letter Z
Vocabulary
zebra
zebu
zero
zest
zigzag
zip
zipper
ziti
zone
zoo
zoom
zucchini

·····Letter Zz·····

Letter Shaping

ACTIVITIES FOR Any Letter

Use these activities to explore the name, shape, or sound of any letter.

What You Will Need

large index cards
letter cards that show both uppercase and lowercase letters
markers
modeling clay, pipe cleaners, or another modeling material

What to Do

- Use a large index card and a marker to make a letter card with both the uppercase and lowercase letters on it (for example, the letter card Cc). Start with a letter that is meaningful to your child, such as first letter of her name or the name of something familiar, such as a family pet.
- Help your child trace both the uppercase C and lowercase c letters on the card and then draw the letters in the air.
- If the uppercase and lowercase letters have the same shape, as is the case with the letter C, point that out.
- Ask your child to use clay, pipe cleaners, or another modeling material to make the shape of the letter C.
- As you look at the shape of each letter and as the child shapes the letters, encourage her to describe the shape of the letters.

Click the Mouse!
**For more letter fun, check out
pbskids.org/lions/gryphonhouse.**
Song: **Upper and Lowercase**
Game: **ABCD Watermelon**

Letter Match

What You Will Need

alphabet chart

alphabet letter cards

Note: Purchase a set of letter cards, such as *LION LETTERS: Alphabet Card Game,* or make your own with index cards and markers.

plastic uppercase letters

What to Do

- On a table, arrange a few plastic uppercase letters, including the first letter in your child's name.
- Give your child a letter card with the first letter of his name.
- Ask your child to hunt for the plastic letter that matches the letter on his letter card. Congratulate him when he matches the letter.
- Ask your child to trace the plastic letter with his fingers. As the child traces the letter, encourage him to say the name of the letter and to describe how the letter looks. Ask, *Does it have straight lines, slanted lines, curvy lines, or circles?*

Another Idea

Suggest that your child repeat aloud the first letter in his name. Tell the child the sound that the letter makes. *Miguel, your name begins with the letter M. The letter M makes the /m/ sound. Let's say it together—/m/. Your friends Mona and Michael have names that also begin with the /m/ sound!*

Click the Mouse!

For more letter fun, check out pbskids.org/lions/gryphonhouse.

Game: Monkey Match

Aa

apple

ACTIVITIES FOR
Any
Letter

Alphabet
Sponges

What You Will Need

alphabet books
alphabet chart
alphabet stamps or sponges
paint
paper

What to Do

- Cut out squares of paper.
- Arrange the cut-out squares of paper, alphabet sponges, and paint on a table.
- Show your child how to press an alphabet stamp or sponge into the paint and then onto the paper to make a letter.
- Your child can choose letters randomly or select the letter sponges that spell her first name.
- Talk to your child about the letters. Help your child identify the names of all the letters on her paper.

For more letter fun, check out
pbskids.org/lions/gryphonhouse.
Game: ABCD Watermelon

"I Spy" the Letter

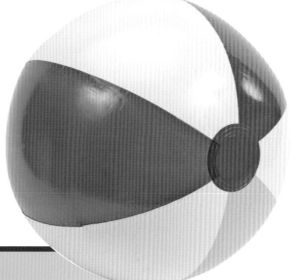

What You Will Need

no materials needed

What to Do

Note: The example used in this activity is the letter
B, but you can use this technique with any letter
of the alphabet.

- Focus on one letter of the alphabet, such as the
letter B. Review the sound that the letter makes.
The letter B makes the /b/ sound.

- Choose a nearby object that begins with that letter. Describe it,
emphasizing the sound the letter makes. For example:
  - *I spy something that is round and begins with the /b/ sound.* (ball)
  - *I spy something that is used to build things and begins with the /b/ sound.* (block)
  - *I spy something that flies in the sky, lives in a nest, and begins with the /b/ sound.* (bird)

Click the Mouse!
For more letter fun, check out
pbskids.org/lions/gryphonhouse.
Game: Theo's Puzzles

Find a Letter

ACTIVITIES FOR
Any Letter

What You Will Need

cookie sheet

letter cards, each showing both the uppercase and lowercase letters

plastic, magnetic uppercase and lowercase letters

two boxes

Note: The letter used in this activity is the letter F, but you can play this game with any letter of the alphabet.

What to Do

■ Show your child a cookie sheet and two boxes, one containing plastic, magnetic uppercase letters (including the focus letter) and one containing lowercase letters.

■ Point to the letter card and say, *This card shows an uppercase F and a lowercase f. In the box, there are some big or uppercase letters. We're going to find all the uppercase F letters and put them on the left side of the cookie sheet. We'll put* *all the other letters here on the right side of the cookie sheet.*

■ As you take the letters out of the box, comment on their shapes. *This letter has one long straight line and two short straight lines. It looks just like the letter F on our letter card. Where on the cookie sheet should I put it?*

■ Choose another letter and talk about how its shape is different from the target letter.

■ Help your child identify the sorted letters by name.

■ Repeat the process as you search the lowercase letter box for the letter f.

Letter Shape Sort

What You Will Need

bag
marker
plastic letters
tray or paper

What to Do

■ Place plastic letters F, H, T, C, S, and O in a bag.

■ Divide a piece of paper in half by drawing a line down the middle.

■ Draw a vertical straight line at the top of the left side and a vertical curved line at the top of the right side.

■ Explain to your child that if a letter has straight lines, it belongs on the side with the straight line, and that if the letter has curved lines, it belongs on the side with the curved line.

■ Have your child take one letter out of the bag at a time, look at it, and decide where to place it on the paper. Think aloud as you model the activity. *Let's take a good look at the letter T. Move your finger along the lines. Are the lines curvy? Are they straight? I see a straight line here and another there. The letter T has two straight lines, so it goes on this side of the paper with the straight line.*

Another Idea

When your child is successful sorting F, H, T, C, S, and O, place letters E, L, I, B, D, and P in a bag. Draw a line down the middle of a piece of paper, creating two columns on the paper. Draw a vertical straight line at the top of the column on the left and both a vertical straight and curvy line at the top of the column on the right. Use these two columns to sort the letters, placing letters that have only straight lines in the left column and letters that have straight and curved lines in the right column. Take one letter out of the bag at a time, look at it, and decide where to place it. For example, pull a letter out of the bag and say, *Where am I going to place this letter L? The letter L has a straight line here and another one here. It has two straight lines and no curvy lines, so I will place it on this side of the paper with just a straight line.*

Click the Mouse!
For more letter fun, check out pbskids.org/lions/gryphonhouse.
Game: ABCD Watermelon

ACTIVITIES FOR
Any Letter

Letter Search and Collage

What You Will Need

construction paper
glue
letter cards
magazine and newspaper pages with
   large type
markers
scissors
store flyers

What to Do

Note: The letter used in this activity is the letter T, but you can do this activity with any letter of the alphabet.

■ Have your child search the headlines of flyers and magazine and newspaper pages for the uppercase T and lowercase t. Tell your child to circle all the letters he finds with a marker.

■ Use a thick marker to write an uppercase T and a lowercase t at the top of a piece of construction paper.

■ Help your child cut out the letters that he found and glue them onto the construction paper.

■ Describe and talk about the difference between the uppercase T and the lowercase t.

For more letter fun, check out
pbskids.org/lions/gryphonhouse.
      Song: Upper and Lowercase
      Game: Sky Riding

Letter Detectives

What You Will Need

flashlight

letter cards or wooden alphabet blocks

What to Do

- Hang or tape letter cards onto the walls or place wooden alphabet blocks throughout the room.
- Dim the lights.
- Tell your child that she is going to be a letter detective. When you count down, she will use the flashlight to find a letter.
- Count down: 3, 2, 1, and then have your child shine the flashlight around the room to look for a letter. Ask her to name each letter each time she finds one with the flashlight.

Click the Mouse!

**For more letter fun, check out
pbskids.org/lions/gryphonhouse.
Game: Sky Riding**

Silly Sound Sentence Story

What You Will Need

markers
objects, or pictures of objects, that all
begin with the same letter
paper

Note: The sound in this activity is the /p/
sound, but you can play this game with
any letter sound.

What to Do

- Display a variety of objects that begin with the /p/ sound; for example, a pink pig, and pictures of pizza and of popcorn.
- Tell your child that you are going to write a silly story using the objects.
- Ask your child to select three or more objects. Then ask him to think of one or two sentences about the selected objects. For example, "The pink pig ate pizza with popcorn on top!"
- Repeat the sentence as you write it on a sheet of paper. Arrange the selected objects (or pictures) in front of you in the order in which they appear in the silly sentence. As you write, point to or pick up the corresponding object (or picture).
- Point to each word as you read the sentence aloud. Congratulate your child on his silly story.
- Point to the objects in front of you. Say, *I notice something about the way these words sound. They all begin with the same sound. Say the words with me—pink, pig, pizza, popcorn. What sound do you hear?* (the /p/ sound)

Click the Mouse!
For more letter fun, check out pbskids.org/lions/gryphonhouse.
Video Clips: Tongue Twister: Choppers Chop, Shoppers Shop
Tongue Twister: This Is the Sixth Sister

Index

Index